# LEMON PIE AND DOG SPIT

By Nancy Bond

**Hedgehog Press**
An imprint of Story Bridges Press
Oakland, CA

ISBN Hardcover 978-0-9887631-3-5

Text and Cover Design by Uniquely Perfect
www.uniquelyperfect.com

Copyright © 2018 Nancy Bond

All rights reserved. No part of this publication may be reproduced, stored in a retrieval system, or transmitted in any form or by any means, electronic, mechanical, photocopying, recording, or otherwise, without the prior permission of the publisher.

Printed in the United States of America

The paper used in this publication meets the minium requirements of American National Standard for Information Sciences—Permanence of Paper for Printed Library Materials, ANSI/NISO X39-48-1992.

DEDICATED TO ALL the teachers in our family and to all those children, teachers, and counselors whom I will never have the pleasure of meeting.

For all teachers, parents and counselors choosing to use this book, I hope it will help you to enable your students to express their thoughts, live up to their fears, obtain a greater understanding of their uncertainties, rejoice in their happiness and just plain laugh with delight.

The poems in this book include:
- Light verse
- Acrostic
- Haiku
- Cinquain
- List poem
- Sonnet
- Ode
- Straight Rhyme
- Incantation
- Modified anaphora

Or at least my interpretation of them! SO THERE.

To children reading this, just have fun.

# MY SOFT WHITE BLANKET

The snow fell softly all the night,
When I awoke the ground was white.

The backyard where I flew my kite,
A fairyland, so sparkling bright!

My eyes a-dance—a wondrous sight.
Do I go out? I think I might.

# ALYSSA'S ON THE MOVE

Dad said to me the other day
We have to move quite far away.

We'll pack our things and head on out
Your toys will go in boxes stout.

The movers come next week at noon
We'll take our things from every room.

I start to sniffle, then to bawl
Don't worry he said – it's not bad at all.

We're going where it's warm and nice
We'll get away from all this ice.

But no, I snuffle, I like the snow
Don't argue he says, we have to go.

Goodbye to friends all over town
When I leave, will you come down?

It's just down south, not far away
The weather's nice, we'll play all day.

They gave me hugs, a party too
A cake, some games, and pictures they drew.

I may have to go 'cuz dad said so
But I'll never forget the places I know.

The old climbing tree out front in the grass
Will be a hiding place for some other lass.

Or the puppies next door in my friend's front yard
Leaving them will really be hard.

When we drive away I'll wave to my school
And no tears now 'cuz that's the new rule.

My new home is sunny and probably big
With plenty of room for my guinea pig.

The neighbors next door will smile and say
Welcome, Alyssa, we hope you will stay.

I'll go to a tree in our very own yard
Picking oranges and grapefruit won't even be hard.

My new school will smell good and kids will be nice
They'll have party cake and I'll get a big slice.

It's going to work, I just know it will
Like sweet lemonade, not some bitter pill.

My eyes are dry, there're no more tears
I'll make new friends and stay there for years.

# CHRISTA PUTS ON A BRAVE FACE

I got really sick just the other day
I think I shared Annie's flu bug.
Mom took my temp, looked worried and said
Christa Jo, it's your day for bed!

Then she hurried off and away to the phone
And I heard her talking so worriedly,
"She's feverish and grumpy with an upset tummy.
She and Annie got a little too chummy."

I listened to her and blew my nose
Snuggled the heating pad tighter.
Hot and cold I shivered and shook
Too sick to even like reading my book.

I knew just what the next step would be
And it wasn't a pleasant thought.
Vicks in my nose and a throw-up pot
Then would come that bad, dreaded shot!

In a couple of days I'll feel good again
Eating french toast and reading my book
Put away Vicks and also that pot
Just a sore bottom from that bad, dreaded shot!

# Dirty Socks and the Missing Cat

The day was dark and dreary
when Mom popped in to say
Wake up! Wake up! You sleepyhead!
Today is room cleaning day!
Look around and what you see
goes on hangars - right in there.
Wash all socks and underpants.
They aren't fit to wear!

Bed needs changing, what a mess
sheets are grimy. Phew! They reek.
Under there you'll no doubt find,
the missing cat, gone now a week!

Then your bathroom needs a scrub
Use cleanser by the sink!
All those words - too much! Too much!
Does she mean it? I don't think.

Mom gets this way from time to time
but I can wait her out.
I'll do what Dad does and pretend
I'm too laid up with gout!

# SHOULD I?

The rain comes down despite my frown
It fills the street and means wet feet
When I go out to play.

There's a lake by the neighbor's gate
Just right to sail or dip my pail
When I go out to play.

Then like a flash, a robin's splash
He's taking a bath in what was the path
As he goes out to play.

Better him than you, warns Mom.

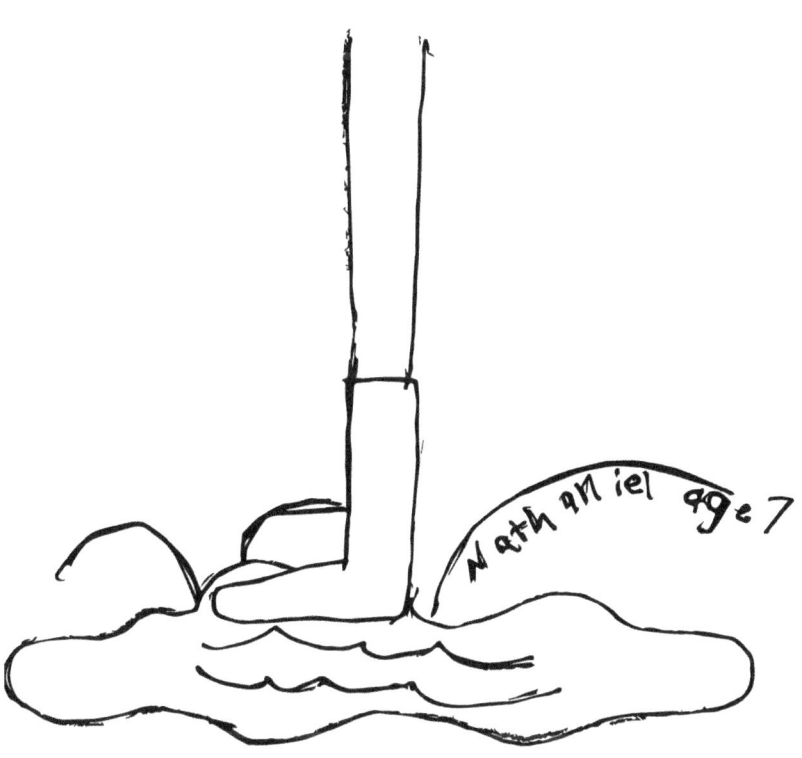

# CHRISTMAS CONFUSION

Christmas is coming!
Mom says if everyone works together
we'll get all the jobs done.

I decide to help decorate.
The tree is extra tall and I fall
right into the middle of it
as I'm hanging the ornaments.
"Better do something else!" she cries.

During the cookie baking
I'm in charge of the sugar.
The recipe says to put in two cups
but I think four would taste better.
"Better do something else!" she says.

How about some lively music?
I choose my favorite CD –
Centipede Plays the Christmas Drums
And Happy Holiday with Elfie and the Wildcats.
"Better play something else!" she warns.

Guess I'll read to little brother.
I show him reindeer on the roof
and a fat man dropping out of the fireplace.
He starts screaming and Mom rushes in.
"Better do something else," she sighs.

So, I go to my chair and I sit
looking out the window at the snow.
When she sees me she snaps,
"Didn't I say we all had jobs to do?
Why are you sitting around?"

I'd like to help
but I just don't know what to do.
I can't seem to figure Mom out.

Rigo
age 15

Sister's in the kitchen
Popping popcorn for me
Pretty soon I smell...
Burned popcorn

# HAROLD SPOILS CHRISTMAS

My Mom and Dad
invited some relatives over
on Christmas Eve.
All the kids played and had fun
except, that is, for Harold.

As soon as he came in the door
the cat took off for under the bed,
remembering the tail pulling
on my birthday, I'm sure.
Harold did it.

We looked at all the presents
trying to guess what was inside.
Harold sneaked my biggest one off,
hid behind the sofa and opened it.
MY PRESENT! HAROLD!

While we were watching a Christmas show
Harold went off on his own.
Soon, from the living room
"What did you do?" shouted Auntie Sue.
Harold shorted out all the Christmas tree lights!

Then it was time for peppermint ice cream.
Mom looked into the freezer —no ice cream!
The empty carton turned up in the bathroom.
Harold took it off where he wouldn't be bothered
and ate it all! Greedy Harold!

At last, thank goodness,
it was time for everyone to leave.
The cat hid under the bed all night,
I knew what my present was and we didn't get ice cream.
No Merry Christmas for Harold again this year!

# THANK YOU, GRAMMY

Writing a thank you note
is a very big job.
I sit and chew my fingers
just thinking about it.

So, should I say thank you
for the ugly Christmas sweater?
Pretending and promising
to wear it to school every Monday.

Which would fit my Monday mood
because Monday's usually a bad day
so I might as well wear it
and make a bad day even worse.

Or should I say how I really feel,
which is to give it to the dog for a bed,
or send it off to the Goodwill Store,
or maybe, exchange it for what I really want-a little snake!

Now that would be an awesome present!
One I'd be glad to thank Grammy for.
Homer could go to school with me
all curled up in my shirt pocket.

Wow, that would be perfect – but –
instead it's an ugly Christmas sweater.
So, chew fingers again and get this over with.
No two ways about it, start writing.

Dear Grammy Laurie,

Hey, Patti up the street
Easy to like you
Attention on me, please
Roaring my love by
Teasing you.

Excitement all day
Coloring hearts in secret
Too much giggling says teacher

Hold your breath
Valentines are being passed
Surely one is mine

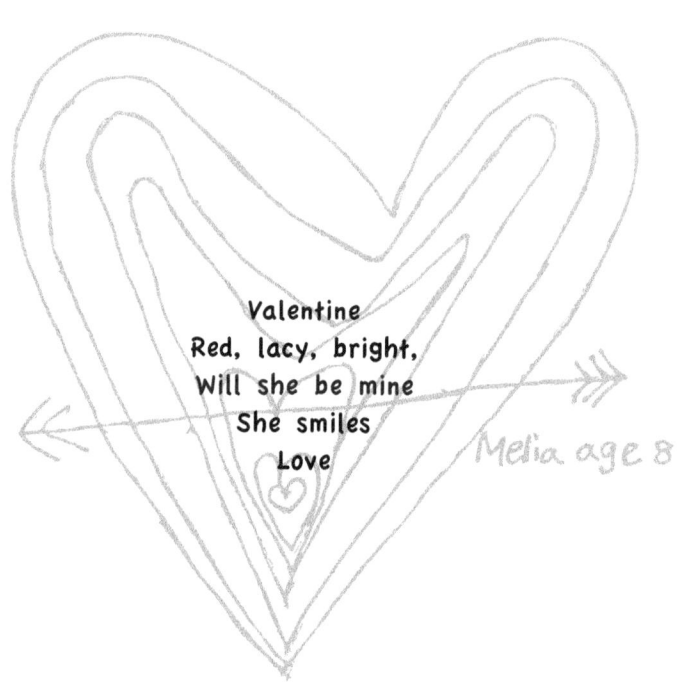

Valentine
Red, lacy, bright,
Will she be mine
She smiles
Love

Melia age 8

# LOVE FROM GUESS WHO

I can hardly wait for Valentine's Day!
It's much better than Christmas
With all the secret messages that say
"Love from guess who?"

I think I know who "love from guess who" is.
Behind me, third row back, second from left,
That cute boy who knows all the answers.
I'll just peek back and see if he's looking at me.

Sure enough, he's smiling and looking at ..
That girl across the aisle! Well, that's disgusting!
I didn't like him anyway.
He probably wouldn't even send a nice valentine!

Now who would send a nice valentine?
I'll look around and see... hmm, There's a cute boy
Sitting up front with no girls around.
I'll bet he ...

Lindsey age 9

# HAROLD SPOILS VALENTINE'S DAY

This should be the best day
of the whole entire year!
VALENTINE'S DAY!
We're all excited
about keeping secrets.
I planned to surprise the cute girl
just down the row.
But then, along came Cousin Harold.

He acts so dumb sometimes.
Scratch that—all the time.
He snooped in my stuff, of course
and found my Valentine surprise.
He let out a huge cackle,
made slobbery kissie noises,
and said he'd tell the cute girl
just down the row!

Harold grabbed my card,
waved it high in the air
just out of my reach.
He pulled off the candy heart,
The one that said heart breaker,
And ate it right in front of me
and the cute girl
just down the row!

Our teacher saw the whole thing
and ordered Harold to her desk.
He handed over the valentine, looking innocent.
As usual.
Then out the door, headed for the principal.
We all smiled and thought 'good riddance.'
Even the cute girl
just down the row!

Racing through puddles
All over wet
Into the house
Now I'm in trouble

# LOOKING GLASS TRUTH

In the looking glass I see
The person that is really me.
Long brown hair and snubby nose,
A yellow shirt with a big pink rose.

Knobby knees that don't quite meet
Rumply socks and giant feet
Shiny shoes with clean shoelaces.
And my teeth—please, no more braces.

Stick out ears that I can't hide,
My smile is even way too wide.
Plain brown eyes with stubby lashes,
Ugly marks from chicken pox rashes.

Why can't I look in there and see
The beautiful princess I want to be?
Shoes that sparkle, a fluffy pink dress.
Gosh, all I see is one big mess!

But my mom just says to me,
"It's important that you see
The kindness you may show a friend
Is better than pretty in the end."

Lindsey
age 9

# MY DOG IS A BIG OLD THING

My dog is a big old thing.
His eyes are brown and his tongue is pink.
And he loves me a lot.
My dog has such thick fur.
A nice, soft pillow that breathes.
And he loves me a lot.

My dog has a nice doggy smell.
But I understand – it's a dog thing.
And he loves me a lot.

My dog comes every time I call.
Even when he's tired and sleepy.
And he loves me a lot.

My dog barks away the scary sounds
When we are home alone.
And he loves me a lot.

My dog sleeps with me at night
So the monster under the bed won't get me.
And he loves me a lot.

Oh, Barney, I'll always take you for walks and give you treats.
I'll give you hugs and sit with you if you're sick or scared.
    Because I love you a lot.

# YOU'RE KIDDING! A BABY??

A new baby is coming
I'm really upset
What this means for me
I'd sooner forget.

Mom will be busy
No walks in the park.
No looking at stars
When it has turned dark.

My special pancakes
No more will be mine.
For Baby, it seems,
Will take all of her time.

This may even mean
No lunchbox treats now.
No chocolate surprises
No yummy brown cow.

Am I liking this?
Not one little bit!
I may just fall down
Throw a VERY BIG fit!

# TOO MANY SPIDERS

I'm trying to like spiders
but it's not coming easy.
They aren't soft and cuddly
and they move way too fast.
Their eyes watch me.

There's this one spider—
big as my hand and hairy all over.
A tarantula.
People keep them for pets!
Now that IS scary.

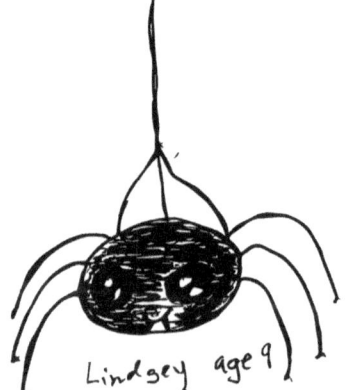

There's one that hangs in corners,
a spindly, long legged Daddy Long Legs.
It's okay, but not hanging over me,
dangling from my bedroom ceiling.
Mom takes it outside.

I absolutely don't want to meet
A scary, shiny Black Widow!
I've only seen pictures but
she looks mean and jumpy.
Hungry and unfriendly.

Dad hoses under the eaves of the house
washing out garden spiders.
They worry me because they're fat,
as big as marbles.
Dad says they won't hurt me.

I know spiders help us—
my arthropod book says so.
It's good they eat insects and not me.
But...how do they know the difference?
It's very worrisome.

Soon, I hope
I'll stop coughing
Can't go outside
Keep away from everyone.

# HAROLD SPOILS MY BIRTHDAY

My birthday party—so awesome!
I invited school friends and neighbors
then Mom reminded me
to ask Cousin Harold.
What was she thinking?

This year my party had a theme.
It was an animal food party.
Everyone brought dog and cat food
but Harold came with canned peas!
What was he thinking?!

Mom's friend from Animal Aid was there
with dogs, cats, and birds to share.
Harold grabbed the cat and pulled his tail!
Well, that set off a terrible howling!
What was he thinking?!

The cat ran off and hid himself
where Harold couldn't go
while Harold clutched his scratched up arm
howling louder than the cat!
What was he thinking?!

Of course this set the dog to barking,
the rabbit twitched and cowered
the parrot squawked out loudly—STOP
and Mom rushed in to see what happened!
What must she be thinking?

Then we all sat down to cake.
I made a wish and then—
Harold blew out my candles!
before I could even take a breath!
What was he thinking?!

Then Mom spoke in her no nonsense voice
"It's time to go," and the animal lady happily sighed
as Harold pushed his way out first
forgetting to take his canned peas with him.
Not thinking again, as usual.

But wait—the best thing of all—
the cat wouldn't come out from hiding
so my coolest present was a new cat!
Maybe Harold has his uses after all.

# WRONG SIDE? RIGHT SIDE? SO WHAT!

Today
my mom said
I got up on the wrong side of the bed.
So I go back to bed
and get out on the other side
but I don't feel any different.
I wonder what she means?

# BALLS OR BOOKS?

Everyone talks about sports.
My friends all like to play.
They think I should, too.
A decision I'll have to weigh.

I thought on playing tennis.
But the ball went so darned fast!
When I got my racquet up
It had whizzed right past!

Basketball—is it my game?
I could dribble if I tried.
Then aim and shoot and—miss.
That hoop is just too high.

Maybe football is for me.
Dressed up in pads and cleats.
Actually, they hit too hard.
It could be grass I'd eat!

Golf seemed a real good sport,
Just hit that little ball.
Oops! My neighbor's window!
This game's not good at all.

The game of baseball looked like fun.
Right by me that ball screamed.
The umpire yelled STRIKE THREE, you're out!
The pitcher stood and beamed.

OK. DECISION TIME!

I am definitely not a sports person.
What I want is a bunch of books.
I'll read all day 'cuz that's my way
To get me off the hook.

# WHEN I GROW UP

When I grow up
   I'll be an ice skater
   Who whirls and jumps
   And never falls.

When I grow up
   I could be a nurse,
   Fixing bumps and cuts
   For kids like me.

When I grow up
   I might own a beauty shop.
   I'll call it Heavenly Hair
   And make ladies beautiful.

When I grow up
   Maybe I'll paint pictures
   Of happy families playing,
   Having picnics in the yard.

When I grow up
   I could be a doctor like mom.
   Except that she's gone a lot.
   On second thought, not a doctor.

When I grow up
   An astronaut would be cool.
   Rocketing to the space station,
   Taking pictures of the world.

When I grow up
   Being a teacher might be fun.
   But not a bossy principal
   Who makes you do timeout.

When I grow up
    I might be a veterinarian
    Taking care of pot bellied pigs,
    So they quit squealing.

When I grow up
    I bet I could be an actor.
    Maybe even a movie star
    Flying around like Peter Pan!

When I grow up
    Being a counselor is awesome.
    They help you understand yourself
    So you play without fights.

When I grow up
    A policeman would be exciting.
    Maybe a little too exciting.
    I don't like guns.

When I grow up
    I'll have lots of choices
    And lots of time to think about them.
    Exciting times ahead for me!

Lindsey age 9

Falling from the sky
the gentle rain brings
cats and dogs.

# CHASING CATS IN RED STRAW HATS

Three pink worms in blue tutus,
Three fat birds in gold mumus,
Three sly cats in red straw hats,
Three black dogs in flowered spats,
Went walking on a sunny day.
The three fat birds eyed the tasty worms,
And they disappeared, each one in turn.
The three black dogs then took off their spats,
The better to chase those three sly cats.
With barking and nipping those three black dogs
Chased those sly cats to a big hollow log.
The red straw hats sailed into the air,
And the dogs grabbed them up without a care.
They put them on, together with spats,
And continued their walk in red straw hats.

Rigo
age 15

# LET'S WORK TOGETHER

To make our family work and not fight
I have jobs I don't really like.
Take out the garbage when it is night
Reset the table, fix it just right
So we can have breakfast when it is light.
Start the dishwasher, be sure that it's tight
A lake on the floor is a terrible plight.
Put out my clothes, hang them in sight
Get my new shoes, the ones that are white.
Mom tucks me in with a smile that is bright
Then says some words that give me a fright.
Sweet dreams, honey, you just sleep tight
Don't let those pinchy old bedbugs bite!

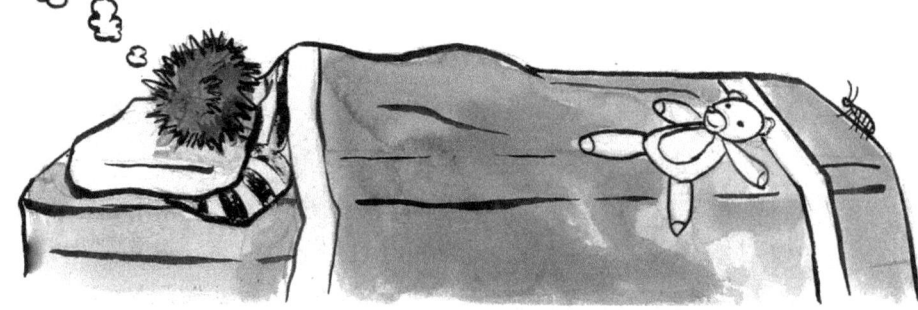

# THE ANIMALS PLAY MARBLES

Four white ducks in big green hats,
Four black cats with crimson spats,
Four red dogs with big white teeth,
Four pink parrots with yellow beaks,
Went to play with twelve young rabbits,
All of whom had very bad habits.
Picking up marbles just for fun,
Marbles they had not even won.
They cheated, you see—oh my, oh me,
Which all the animals could plainly see.
So they picked their marbles from off the floor,
And marched quite smartly out the door.

# HAROLD SPOILS EASTER

Mom's awesome idea—an Easter party!
We can hunt eggs and invite the Easter Bunny.
All our friends and cousins can come
and, unfortunately, this also means Cousin Harold.

The big day finally arrives!
Colored eggs are hiding all over the yard
and the Easter Bunny hops in to hand out candies.
All of us kids hop around, too, waiting for the GO signal.

Then the gate slams open and in runs Harold, late,
shouting "Wait for me" as he pushes to the front
just as the bell dings GO.
Straight off he runs, shoving his way to the easy eggs
trampling marshmallow bunnies along the way.

Then he sneaks up behind the Easter Bunny,
grabs his tail and jerks it off!
He tosses the furry ball into the air and cackles
as the Bunny feels a breeze on his back side!
The Bunny stops saying "Happy Easter, honey"
and instead mutters, "He's a menace."
I know he means Harold and not Dennis.

Auntie Sue and Mom hear the screaming.
Auntie grabs Harold while Mom hugs the girls.
It is all too much for the cat
who runs up the apple tree.
Harold gets dragged off to be in timeout
under the same tree.
I sort of thought it would serve him right
if the cat dropped down on his slobbery, crying face!

He never gets to come back
so we count our eggs in peace
and eat the chocolate rabbits and jelly beans.
I move so he can see how much
I like what I am eating.
Mom pins the tail back on the Bunny
and he stays away from the apple tree.
I finally take Harold a cookie.
Which he just throws back at me.
Auntie Sue tells him to get over his attitude
or he won't have any friends.

I'd say Amen to that because
I'm ready to unfriend him.
From now on I think I'm just going to have
secret parties so he won't come.
It'd be way more peaceful
and the cat would like it, too.

# SINK OR SWIM

Swimming lesson time soon.
I am not happy about this.
What if I can't touch bottom?
What if my nose fills with water
What if my teacher lets go of me

And I sink to the bottom!

I think I'll go live at Davy's house
until swimming lesson time is over.

Lindsey age 9

# TANGLED WITH THE DOG

I had a wreck the other day
My bike is quite a mess.
The neighbor's dog got in my way
He truly is a pest!

I went south, the bike went north
The dog just stood and looked
His tongue hung out, his eyes were sad
He knew my goose was cooked!

The horn was cracked and also crooked
The front wheel bent clear out
Our door flew open, here came Mom,
Waved her arms and gave a shout!

It was the dog she rushed right to
Crooned and called him "my sweet pup"
Didn't spare a glance MY way
And here it's me that's all beat up!

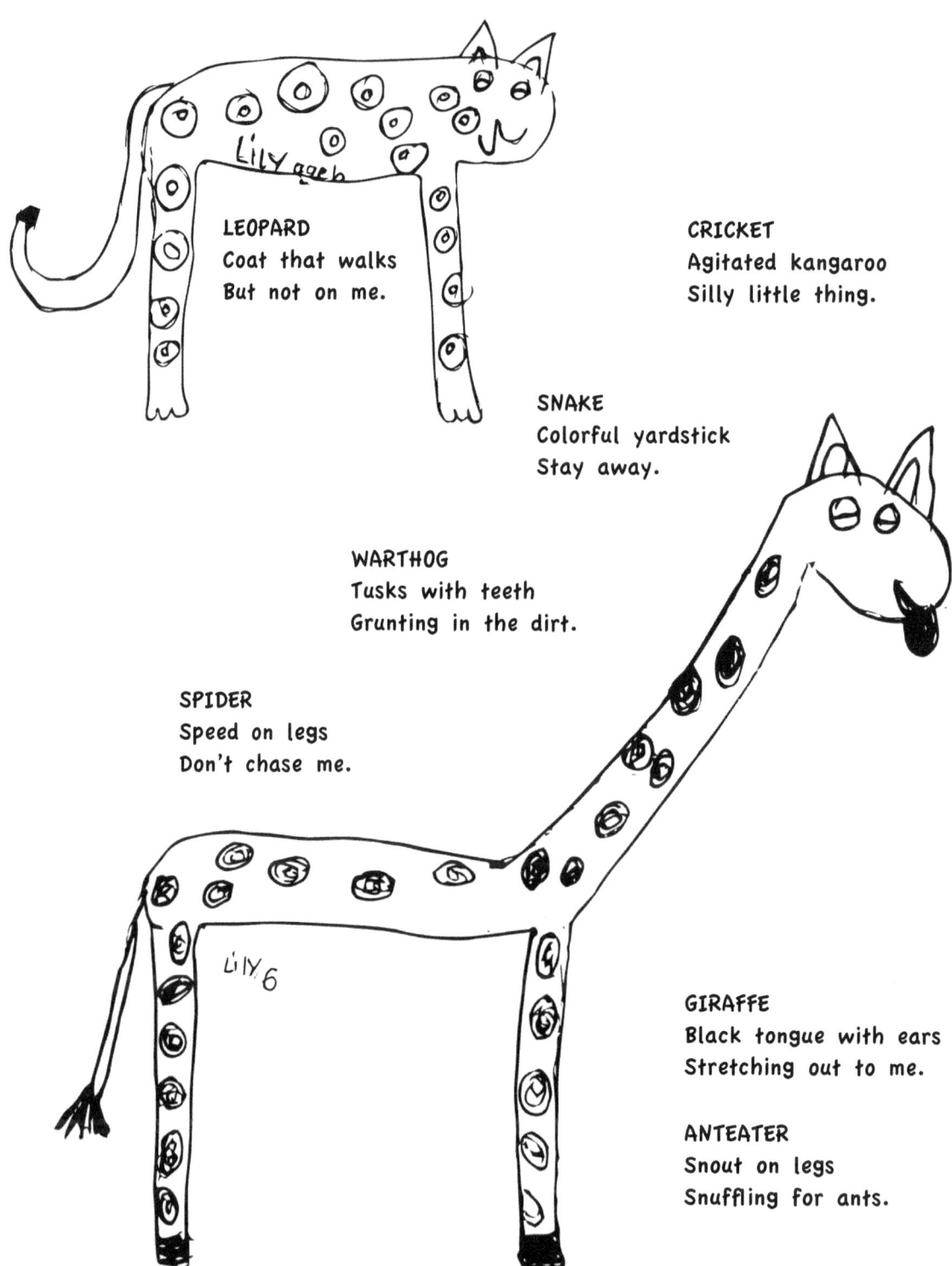

**LEOPARD**
Coat that walks
But not on me.

**CRICKET**
Agitated kangaroo
Silly little thing.

**SNAKE**
Colorful yardstick
Stay away.

**WARTHOG**
Tusks with teeth
Grunting in the dirt.

**SPIDER**
Speed on legs
Don't chase me.

**GIRAFFE**
Black tongue with ears
Stretching out to me.

**ANTEATER**
Snout on legs
Snuffling for ants.

**LION**
Mane with a roar
Looking hungry.

**PENGUIN**
Pompous little dress up
Without a party.

**RACCOON**
Burglar in the night
Stealing the dog's food.

# WISHFUL THINKING

I wish for a horse with all my heart.
He'll be brown with a long gold tail
that streams behind as I ride like the wind.

Over the field, past the white rail fence
while the cows watch and, tails up, give chase.
To the ends of the earth we will run
or at least as far as the fence lets us.

I'll pat his neck and tell him to jump
and with tail and mane flying we'll jump over that fence.
Then we're off on our own!

Two explorers ready for the race track or circus
where we will be stars and never have to take out the garbage.
It'll just be me and my horse—all alone forever.

Or at least 'till dinner
when my mom says I have to be home.

Ice cream cone of green
peppermint I know
a big lick of
BROCCOLI

# IT'S RAINING IN THE DOWNSTAIRS CLOSET

I'm in timeout
Not sure of the reason.
Maybe it's the dog
I was just sort of teasin'.

It could be the flowers
I flattened to smush.
My bike wheel got stuck
Near the biggest rose bush.

Perhaps it's the shirt
I got covered with paint.
Mom was unhappy
I thought she might faint!

It could have been Laurie
My sister, of course.
She hid my Jets poster
I yelled myself hoarse.

But mostly, I think
It would be the water.
I turned on the tub
Then forgot. Bad daughter.

It went over the side
Right onto the floor.
Then it ran sideways
Flowed under the door.

All over the carpet
And down all the cracks,
Right through the ceiling
On the clothes closet racks!

Then there was screeching
Feet running upstairs.
She found me and my book
Curled up in the chair.

So that's it for sure
It must be the reason.
In time out forever.
Mom's NOT sort of teasin'!

Lindsey age 9

# MAPLE PUPPIES

In the bag, my favorite treat—
maple bars—like sleeping puppies
just waiting for someone to hold them.

Slowly my hand goes in
careful not to disturb the luscious sticky
clinging to the sides.

Stealthily out comes a pup,
a soft pillow in a yummy maple pillowcase.
Aah! I float on a maple cloud.

I nibble delicately like a tortoise,
I lick the frosting like a cat.
Then a lion-like bite, one enormous snap!

All gone. How sad. I lick each finger.
But wait—there's one left—so lonesome, all alone.

Maybe...

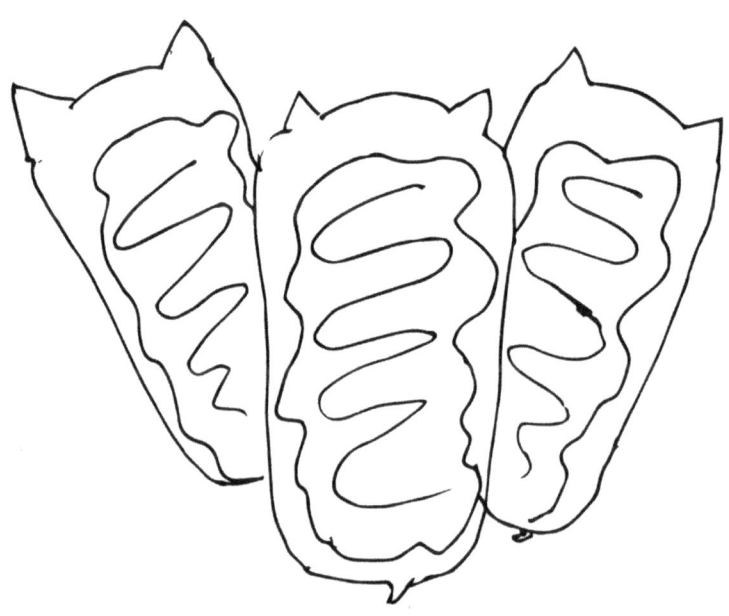

Very soon now
A day we all dream of
Can't wait for June
At last I'm free
Tearing home on my bike
Into the pool every day
On the plane to Disneyland
Now that's my kind of life!

# COLE THINKS TOO MUCH

One day while sitting on the floor
I started thinking.
When I was mad I slammed the door
Maybe I should run away.

One day while sitting on my chair
I started thinking.
I lost my sister's teddy bear
Maybe I should run away.

One day while sitting on my bed
I started thinking.
I went off too long on my sled
Maybe I should run away.

One day while sitting in the car
I started thinking.
I stole cookies, dropped the jar
Maybe I should run away.

One day while sitting on the bus
I started thinking.
Mom said no, I made a fuss
Maybe I should run away.

One day while sitting quietly
I started thinking.
I'll go to mom and say so nicely
I don't want to run away.

She'll grab me up and hug awhile.
Say, "Cole, I need you every day.
We'd be so sad without your smile,
The noisy way you play,
The dirty socks all in a heap.
The slamming doors,
The cookie sneak,
So - how about we go make s'mores!"

One day while sitting happily
I started thinking.
I really love my family
S'mores are good, I think I'll stay!

# LEMON PIE & DOG SPIT

Mom's lemon pie
smelled super delish
      and brought me and my dog to the kitchen.

He sniffed out the pie and drooled on the floor
then, huge leap to the table and gobbled that meringue
      before I could even stop him!

Sissy Pants sister saw and screeched out:
"YUCK! I totally refuse
      to eat slimy dog spit!"

And I just smiled, 'cuz then I knew
that super delish lemon pie
      would be ALL MINE!

# SPYING ON CALEB

The climbing tree in my back yard
Raises its branches and lets me in.
Its leaves gently motion
For me to come aloft
Where the breeze hides.

I can see over the fences and housetops
Keeping a watch out
for anything new and exciting
So I can report at dinnertime
And dad can call me
The Nancy Drew
Of the neighborhood.

The first thing I see is Mrs. Grumpy
Shooing the neighbor's dog that has
Just messed up her lawn.
I smile and cheer.
For the dog.

Mr. Special Delivery comes to Mr. Lonely's house
Bringing a big package.
That's exciting for
Mr. Lonely!

I smile and cheer the postman
But before he's even back on the sidewalk
Mrs. Happy walks by
And waves happily to both
Mrs. Grumpy and Mr. Lonely.

I see she moves quickly to one side of the walk
To make room for my friend Caleb
Who is riding his skateboard
Taking up lots of sidewalk.

Then who should come honking up the street
Waving to all of them?
It's my dad
Home for supper.
So down I climb.
Lots to report on tonight!

# CHARM(ING) RECIPE

Half an ounce of hummingbird
Two teaspoons rotten mash
Enormous blob of bacon grease
Snip of deer's eyelash.

Half a spoon of cat tail fluff
Scales of some green lizard
Stinging nettles, finely chopped
Sliced fresh turkey gizzard.

Cayenne pepper, a big shake
Mix well with castor oil
For color add a few red ants
Then school paste .. And boil.

All together now it's mixed
Simmer slowly, stir it once
At the end of day it's nicely fixed
Just the treat for that big dunce!

    My big brother
    Noisy, annoying
    An odious toad!

# CHOCOLATE CHERRY OR CHUNKY MONKEY?

Eating cold, scrumptious ice cream
is the shivering best thing ever!
In a spoon, a dish or a cone
With my friend or all alone
Let's bring on my favorite treat
Just as much as I can eat!

So many licking good flavors
my eyes dance and my tasters tingle.
Chunky Monkey and Luscious Lime,
Mango Sunrise and Coca Cola Time,
Frutti Parfait, Chocolate Cherry,
Cookies 'N Cream, and Huckleberry.

Loads and loads of choices, but—
"take your time," smiles the scooper.
Eyeing the Mango, I haven't a clue,
that Mocha looks a strange sort of hue,
Luscious Lime—it's just way too green,
Chunky Monkey—now that's a bad scene!

Take a deep breath, point to THAT one
my favorite hides deep in the back.
Two scoops please. Well--make it three.
Coming up now—what'll it be?
My yummy favorite—Vanilla Sky
The very biggest I can buy!

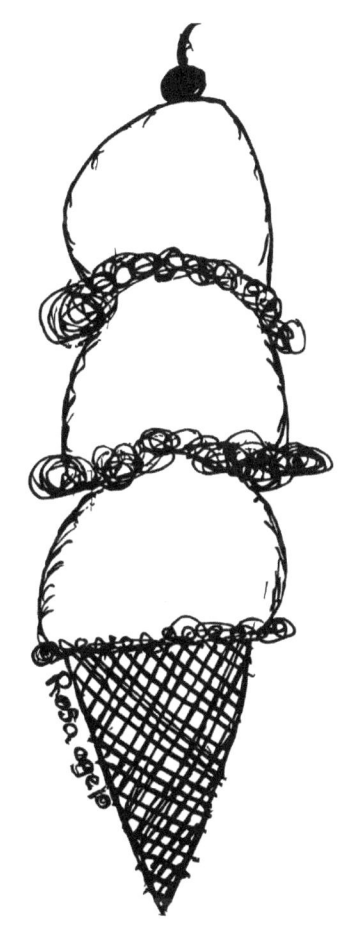

# GRAMMY CAMP

When summer comes
I always know
To Grammy's house
I'll get to go.

She lives across
Ten states from me.
I go by plane
From sea to sea.

When I arrive
She rushes up.
Hugs and kisses!
Grammy Camp, yup!

Then off we go
In her shiny car.
To her big house.
It's not too far.

I race the dog,
I ride the horse.
I will take lots
of baths, of course.

We eat fun food
Hot dogs and chips.
Pancakes for lunch
I smack my lips.

We stay up late
Searching for stars.
Huddled in blankets
Looking for Mars.

On hot afternoons
Off to the pool
Noodles and slides,
It's just sooo cool!

Out in the forest
There's a zipline.
I'm tall enough.
Zipping's sublime.

The Air Museum
Just down the way.
Spruce Goose and slides,
Grammy will pay.

A week has gone
I hug goodbye.
Grammy Camp's over
I leave; big sigh.

There's always another
Summer in store.
Grammy Camp calls.
Can't wait for more!

# MOM ON THE PECK

Mom is on the peck today
Wish I knew just why.
    Perhaps I'll stay out of her way
        And maybe I'll get by.
            But it didn't work that way.

Playing in the dirt today
I got so gloriously grimed.
    Seeing me she shrieked and yelled
        What is that slippery slime??

It's only dirt was my protest
Mixed in with garden water.
    It stuck right on my knees and hair
        Mom, I'll wash, I'm a good daughter.

She marched away and left me there
To think on being bad.
    Just for why, I could not say.
        It made me feel so sad.

When Mom gets mad it's pretty bad
Grounded in my room.
    I'll know next time to sit and read.
        Avoid this doom and gloom.

I was good, stayed by the house
Played nicely in our yard.
    Now I'm being punished.
        Mom on the peck is hard!

    Things don't always work the way you think.

# MY WAY OR MOM'S WAY?

What I like is different than what Mom likes.
I keep finding that out.
Here's some fr' instances.

I like jumping in puddles when it rains,
eating my fill of chocolate cookies,
hiding my broccoli under the bread
and playing video games instead of doing homework.

Leaving frogs in my sister's room,
playing my trumpet good and loud,
never making my bed
and forgetting to take out the garbage.

Now mom has a different view about things.

She doesn't like me wet and muddy,
eating all the dessert and hiding the broccoli.
She thinks homework first and games later.
The bed's a mess and the garbage stinks, she grumbles.
The trumpet's too loud and—
don't let's talk about those frogs!

You need to compromise, she preaches
but I like what I'm doing
"Compromise" would go all her way
I just know it.
I need some help figuring this out!

# BIG BEAUTY

Oh, My Beautiful Pencil Sharpener!
Always ready to entertain me
and sometimes to actually perform your job.
Plugged in and ready to go
making that satisfying grinding sound
chewing away at my pencil
and sometimes my crayon
which you have to spit out
before I use you on pencils again.

Oh, My Hard Working Pencil Sharpener!
Happiest when only I am in the room
giving you the good workout you like.
Chewing first my red pencil, then the blue,
happily mingling shavings to make purple
until your tummy is so totally full
you stop grinding and cough.
An amazing lot of purple spurts out
so I know to empty you now,
seeing with satisfaction all the work we have done!

Look at my chewed up pencils lying in a neat row
in all their inch-long glory
never to be used again
because my pencil sharpener and I
are such a good team
having so much fun!

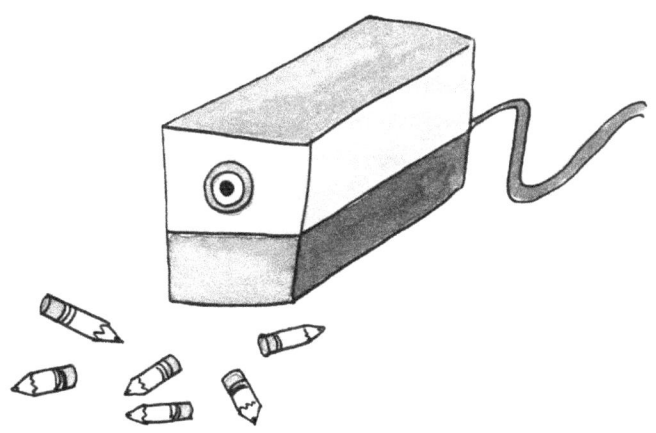

# DON'T BULLY ME!

It's recess—I don't want to go.
There's a kid out there that picks on me.
She calls me names and points and laughs.
She just can't seem to let me be.

I turn around, don't want to hear.
But then she gets right in my face.
Says hurtful words I could not say
as she traps me in that place.

I'll tell my teacher after class.
She helps us all obey the rule.
Because everyone should know by now
There's NO BULLYING IN OUR SCHOOL!

# SPROUTS BELONG IN BRUSSELS (SAYS CASEY)

Brussels sprouts for dinner.
I think I cannot
bear it.

That tossed green salad
isn't my favorite, either.
I think I'll pass.

Bring on that chicken
crispy, crunchy, fried just right.
Three big pieces, please.

There's melted cheese bread
A yummy hunk
will be so scrumptious.

I look away and...what is this?
Brussels sprouts appear
Humongous scaly balls!

Mom's voice says something bad
"Clean plate night, Casey.
Eat it, or else...

No dessert for you tonight."
Chocolate cake with cherry filling
ice cream on the top.

So I slowly eat my dinner.
Gag it down, eyes closed
thinking about the treat

Gooey frosted chocolate cake.
The biggest piece, I hope.
Colored sprinkles, all over.

Tonight I REALLY earned it!

# BREAKFAST RABBIT

My favorite breakfast is a pancake,
but not just a plain pancake.
Mom cuts a hole in the middle,
then cuts the hole part into two pieces
and puts them on top for rabbit ears!
Then she takes two pieces of a cantaloupe slice
and puts them on the bottom for a tasty bow tie.
We make syrup whiskers and M&M eyes,
then slide a fried egg in that empty hole.
Mom calls this Well Balanced, I call it
Egg In The Hole!
But Dad winks and says,
Rabbit Down The Hatch!

# TOSSING TONSILS

I went to have my tonsils out,
the nurse was kind and nice.
I asked for drinks of water
but she brought me cups of ice.

A nice man came up to my bed,
looked in my mouth and nose.
Then smiled at me real big and said,
"Soon now you'll get to go."

A lady dressed in white and blue
came by, her arms piled high
with quilts for special kids like me.
I'm her favorite guy!

The nurse was kind, the doctor too,
And I fell fast asleep.
Soon awoke for a popsicle treat
And home with a quilt I could keep.

Now I'm feeling really good
my tonsils thrown away.
That special quilt is on my bed
to remind me of that day.

# LIDA ROSE

A kitty came up to our house
one wet and rainy day,
with big blue eyes and long white fur
we decided she should stay.


I was just a little kid
like maybe three or four.
We named the kitty Lida Rose,
she'd meet me at the door.


When I got big and went to school
Rosie stayed at home.
She'd stay and play and scratch the chairs
and would not dare to roam.


When I was sick and down in bed
Lida Rose was there,
curled up right beside my head
paws tangled in my hair.


Then in seventh grade I heard
my parents talking sadly.
Lida Rose was pretty sick
and I felt really badly.


I cuddled her, was extra kind,
Rose didn't want to play.
She'd hide way underneath the bed
and stay throughout the day.

One day when I came home from school,
I knew something was quite wrong.
Mom just hugged me tight and said
Lida Rose is gone.

I began to cry, I couldn't stop.
My sweet kitty was no more.
No soft meows, no gentle pats,
no meeting at the door.

There's a place for my best friend,
somewhere a kitty goes.
So someone else can love and hug
my sweet little Lida Rose.

My fortune cookie
opens to reveal its message:
your face is dirty.

# BEST IN A MESS

Cleaning my room
Is the very best thing
Ever a kid can do
Or so my mom says
But take it from me, it's NOT true!

I know that my socks
Are under the bed.
Both shoes are hiding there, too,
In the very same place I left them
Yesterday when I was through.

My shirt's on the bedpost, along with my cap,
My underwear – looks like it's gone!
Someone's snuck in here, I know
Take it from me, it was Mom.

Thank goodness my baseball
Is still on the floor.
I can see my best bat
Tossed back by the door.

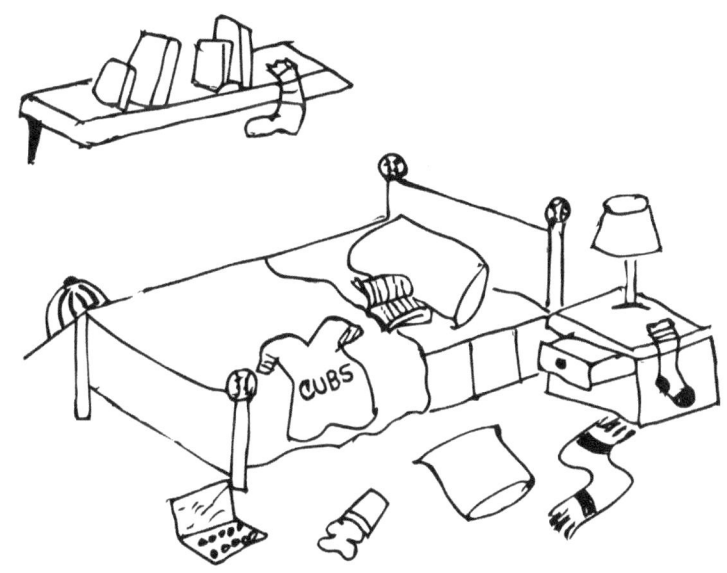

If I had to clean up
I'd never be able
To locate the Legos
I leave on the table.

My mom doesn't know
I have radar feet
And they just won't work
When things are so neat!

But take it from me, it IS true!

# HAROLD SPOILS THANKSGIVING

I wait for Thanksgiving all year
when the house smells like turkey
and pumpkin pie,
and yummy sweet potatoes
soaking in brown sugar and marshmallows.

We get to use the dining room table
and the best dishes
which doesn't matter much to me
'cause turkey tastes great
off a paper plate.

Our family all comes and I like that
except, that is, for Harold
who's my age
and tries to boss me around.
Even in my own house!

We don't have a kids' table, so I'll make sure
Harold sits far away on the end,
while my seat is going to be
next to Auntie Sue and Mom.
And the turkey.

I'll dig in first and take the piece
I know Harold will want!
That'll fix him--I'll take both drumsticks
even if one's all
I can eat.

After all, it IS Thanksgiving
and we can eat all we want even if we get sick
which I did once.
On second thought,
one drumstick is enough.

Then dinner's over and everyone
goes to the living room.
The fireplace is cozy
and the snow is falling
outside.

Everyone talks and laughs.
I think what a nice family
except for Harold, looking green
now throwing up on the carpet.
Too much turkey, no doubt.

I should feel sorry but I don't.
At least no more bossing me today.
But there's always tomorrow,
so maybe ..
we'll negotiate a truce.

That enchanting tooth fairy
silent in the night left me a note:
clean your room.

# ACKNOWLEDGMENTS

I am very much indebted to many people for their contributions to this book. To the faculty and alumni of Harvey Clarke Elementary School, my home away from home for thirty years; to the hundreds of students I am humbled to have walked among who unknowingly provided all the ideas for my poetry by just living their lives with me every day for thirty years. That actually works out to 9,000 days or 63,000 hours! It was an honor to have been able to step into the lives of these young people and share their joys, concerns, and confusions.

To my husband, Ken, for his constant encouragement and relentless optimism; to daughter, Patti, herself a poet, for her excitement, praise and enthusiasm for the project; to son David and daughter in law, Laurie for their valuable time, generous support and encouragement, as well as the gift of much needed insight into the complexities of technology.

To readers, Frances Noble, Mary Jane Nordgren, Helen Yuditsky, Dena Heath, and daughter Lindsey and son Nathaniel, Angela Zusman and daughters Sasha and Lily. Thanks for providing tough love and suggestions.

To my primary illustrator, Emily Lux, who took the poetry and produced exactly the right illustrations and to whom I offer my most sincere thanks and many hugs. She was ably assisted by Lindsey and Nathaniel Heath and friends Malia and Rosa, Rigoberto Ceja, Sasha and Lily Cooney, Suzanne Lucas, and Jane Walter Bousman, who took time from her own art show preparations to assist me.

# ABOUT THE AUTHOR

Nancy grew up in Baker City in Northeastern Oregon. She received a BA from the University of Oregon and an MA and Handicapped Education endorsement from Portland State University. She worked as an elementary classroom teacher for 30 years.

Her work is inspired by the hundreds of elementary students she was privileged to work and laugh with each day for all those years. Now retired, she and her husband divide time between Western Oregon and Southern California. Their lives are enlivened by two grown children, two granddaughters and three great grandsons. Nancy travels, bakes, sings to the flowers and beats the weeds into submission as well as writes childrens books.

www.ingramcontent.com/pod-product-compliance
Lightning Source LLC
Chambersburg PA
CBHW061418090426
42743CB00022B/3483